A Weeping with Me, God?

Martha Bittle Clark

BROADMAN PRESS
Nashville, Tennessee

Dewey Decimal Classification: 248.4
Subject Headings: CONSOLATION // JOY AND SORROW
Library of Congress Catalog Card Number: 86-17194
Printed in the United States of America

All Scripture quotations are taken from the King James Version of the Bible.
The quotation on page 44 is an excerpt from the sermon "The Gospel of Strength in Weakness" by Herman R. Yoos.

Library of Congress Cataloging-in-Publication Data

Clark, Martha Bittle.
  Are you weeping with me, God?

  1. Consolation.   2. Bereavement—Religious aspects—
Christianity.   3. Clark, Sherry—Death and burial.
4. Clark, Martha Bittle.   I. Title.
BV4907.C54   1987   248.8'6'0924 [B]   86-17194
ISBN 0-8054-5436-5

for Herman, who walked with me through every stage of grief

for Cecil, my husband, my love and my most treasured friend

and especially for Sherry

ACKNOWLEDGMENTS

An author is but a single component in the process of publishing a book. My heartfelt thanks are due to those who willingly shared my sorrow and thus helped this book become a reality. Richard Boye was the first to encourage the publication of my journal. William Robertson spent many hours reading and editing my notes. Ann Hoover gave invaluable help in deciding which incidents should be included in the final manuscript. Larry Wick, Tom Wilder, Gwen Rowe, and Blair Robertson offered many useful suggestions. And, of course, no word of thanks could be complete without mentioning my children, who sustained me with their love and understood when I seemed to forget for a while that they were still alive.

Was It Just a Dream?

. . . that I held you in my arms and sang lullabies to
   you,
   touching the curve of your cheek as I rocked gently
   to and fro?

. . . that I watched you take your first shaky steps to Pat,
   losing your balance at the end and toppling into his
   arms?

. . . that you left for kindergarten holding tightly to
   Lisa's hand,
   looking back tearfully at Mama and home and kitty?

. . . that the audience at Ovens gave you a standing
   ovation,
   clapping with delight for the tiniest dancer in the
   show?

. . . that you wept and hid when Mike brought his girl
   home,
   saying we didn't need any more girls around our
   house?

. . . that I watched in surprise as you swam one day,
   seeing not a child, but the glow of a lovely young
   girl?

. . . that we took two weeks to shop for your first long
   dress,
   driving too far and paying too much, to get that
   special one?

. . . that I saw you graduate through unshed tears,
knowing the part of your life that was ours, too,
had now ended?

. . . that we drove you to college and settled you in,
holding you close a moment too long and
wondering what the years would bring?

Oh Sherry, was it just a dream that they told me you
were dead?

It must have been a dream.

I couldn't have borne the living, the loving, and the
losing of you.

Introduction

There was nothing in my life that prepared me for the horror of my child's death. Such an event was as far removed from my way of thinking as being struck by lightning. And yet the call came—the call that all parents fear the most. Our youngest child, eighteen-year-old Sherry, had been killed in an accident. She was a passenger in her roommate's car on the way back to the dorm. No alcohol. Just a rain-slicked road, a curve, and a tree. Mere seconds, but a life was gone and a dream ended for all of us.

I was devastated with grief, and no one could comfort me. What words *can* be said to someone in the midst of such crushing sorrow? Everywhere I looked, people seemed to support the notion that a true Christian praises God in everything that happens, that to die is to rejoice and that grieving is short-lived or selfish. Because of my bitterness and feelings of guilt, I began to believe that I would never see Sherry's face, or that of my Savior's, in heaven. Those were the darkest and loneliest days I have ever known.

I emerged from shock to search through books on grief, sermons on eternal life, and theological publications on faith for some kind of comfort. But in all my searchings, I found no writings to explain my feelings of outrage at a Creator God who would allow such a horrendous tragedy to cut short a life that had hardly begun. The books on grief seemed written by authors who accepted death much more passively than I could. No one spoke of opening a window so God could hear the harsh accusations and cries of anger; no one mentioned that grief hurts in a physical, crushing way; and no one warned that deep despair affected every aspect of life, even one's sexuality. Since earliest childhood, I have thanked God for every blessing in my life, but now I was compelled to ask what part He had played in this cruel accident. Is He responsible for our joys *and* sorrows? And does this make Him the author of evil itself?

Because I have kept a journal for many years, my pain and despair were recorded almost by some innate instinct from the moment I first heard of Sherry's death. Psychologists would suppose it was an effort to grasp control over a life that had somehow spun *out* of control. I only know it was probably the only hold on reality I had during the first few months. From the incoherent thoughts of the first day, when I wasn't sure whether it was Sherry or me who had died, to the sunny day in April nearly ten months later when I was finally able to thank God for her life, the journey through grief was all recorded, inadvertently making a record of a parent's greatest nightmare.

Last summer, as I looked back over the pages, I was struck by my growth as a Christian and by my new understanding of God's place in our sorrow. Why do we suffer? For centuries, humanity has pondered this question. Some would say we are tested, instructed, tempted, and even punished by sorrow. I believe these are but partial views, and each of us has to search for and find our own answers. But for parents struggling with a God who allows horrible things to happen to His children, there should be someone telling them those feelings are normal, those feelings are not bad, and those feelings can lead them into a new beginning where they are victors of a struggle, not mere survivors.

And then I knew. I can be that someone. . . .

Prologue

Surely, there is no journey as lonely, nor one embarked upon with more pain, than the walk a parent takes through the wilderness of grief.

Sherry Clark

She is dead. My little girl is dead. Oh dear God, no. It can't be true. But Cecil said there was an accident last night, and Sherry was killed.

Please, God, couldn't a mistake have been made? Wouldn't I have felt *something* in my sleep if Sherry were dying? I never even felt her leave.

She'll be so scared when she wakes up. I always held her when she was scared. Who's going to hold her now?

This isn't happening. I'll just stay calm and wait. Someone will call soon and tell us it was not Sherry they found in that car. We'll ride to Cullowhee and I can see her, make sure she is all right. *She has to be all right!*

Everyone is talking, talking, talking. I hear the words, but they are coming from such a long way off. I look at faces, but no one looks at me. I am here, but I am not here. Could it be me who has died?

I touch Cecil's arm to be sure he is real. He turns to say that Mike has already left Birmingham to drive home, and Pat has called from the airport in Atlanta. They will be there when we arrive in Charlotte. Brenda has gone to unlock our house and wait for her brothers.

What about Lisa? She is camping and I don't know where. Someone leaves the house to find her. Are they going to tell her that her little sister is dead? She will be so angry if they tell her and it turns out to be a horrible mistake.

The driveway is filling up with cars. How did everyone hear so quickly? Don't they know it might not be true? It *can't* be true!

Norma says that Carrol and Ken are on the way from

11

Spindale to drive us back to Charlotte. But I don't want to leave. I am afraid to go home. What if we find out it is true?

Where are you, Herman? I keep dialing and dialing the church, and there is no answer. I even tried calling you at home. I *need* you. No one else can help. You *must* make God understand how much I love Sherry—and how I *can't* let her go! At least, not yet. Not at eighteen. Not from a wreck that wasn't even her fault.

I am so scared. I put my hands on my knees, but the shaking won't stop. Please, God, let this be a nightmare.

This morning's paper had a picture of Sherry on the front page. A big, heavy paper. It must be Sunday. I read about the accident, but it doesn't make sense. Not any sense at all. That can't be Sherry they're talking about.

The children are home now, but I try not to look at their eyes. The pain I see there makes the nightmare almost real, and I can't bear that kind of horror. Please, won't someone tell me this isn't true?

The rest of the family is beginning to arrive—my father and brothers, Cecil's sisters, our nieces and nephews. I know they want to be here but, if Sherry is dead, what can they do?

The house is filled with people. No one knows what to say, and I don't know what to say, either. I thank them for coming, but it is someone else talking and not me at all. The real me couldn't stand here and be polite with this awful pain crushing my body. Is it too late for you to change your mind, God? Don't take my little girl away.

There are so many flowers and so much food being brought to us. But Sherry cannot smell the flowers or eat the food, and neither can I. I went to her room and touched her bed, her pillow, but I can't feel the touch. I can't feel anything. Sherry and I are both gone.

Herman has stayed with us most of the day, and I am glad. He is my only connection to Sherry and to heaven. He prayed with us and asked you to comfort us in our sorrow. I don't think he knows that my heart is too full of anger to pray to you, myself. I trusted you to watch over her, God, when I could not be there. *Where were you last night? Why did you let her die?*

13

We had to select a casket for Sherry today. A casket for my little girl. My God. How can she be dead? We were laughing with her just the other night. This day, this moment cannot be real.

Lynn and little Erin were waiting for us when we returned home. They had ridden the train all the way from New Orleans to be with us for the funeral. Erin told me Sherry had gone to live with Jesus. Then she stretched out her arms and said, "Jesus loves Sherry *this* much, and He is so glad to see her!"

Part of me envies the faith of this little toddler, but another part of me asks why, if Jesus loved her, did He let her die so young? What has happened to my faith? What has happened to *me?* My anger has turned into rage, and it must show in my eyes. I am afraid to look at anyone. No one could be a Christian and feel such fury.

This afternoon, Herman came to plan the funeral with us. We will sing Sherry's favorite hymn, "Lift High the Cross," when she is carried into her beloved church for the last time. Both the boys' and the girls' basketball teams of UNCC and their coaches will be pallbearers. Her friend David will carry the crucifix, and Lynda and Melody will join her church friends in the choir. We have asked the cheerleaders and her Delta Zeta sisters to sit down front as honorary pallbearers. All the parts of our worship service that she loved will be used—the processional, the banners, and the choir.

Does she know, God? Can she tell how hard we are trying to make everything as she would have chosen? This is the last thing we can ever do for her. *I still can't believe this is happening.* Is this a punishment for loving her too much?

14

They let me see Sherry today. I had begged to be allowed one last look at that lovely little face. Friends warned me against seeing her. They wanted me to remember her the way she was before the accident. Do they think I've never seen her with cuts and bruises?

> (Sherry, Sherry, how like a giver of cheer you looked with your little white pleated skirt and your green and white sweater and your dark curls laying so softly on the pillow. I had to whisper some things in your ear before I kissed you good-bye for the last time. There was so much I never had a chance to tell you. I always thought there would be a tomorrow.)

God, is there someone in heaven who takes time to hold and comfort children and teenagers if they are homesick and confused at first? Could you, by any chance, stay close to her until I come? I'm afraid Sherry will get tired of singing praises after a while and want to come home.

It was like being part of a nightmare to ride in that funeral limousine. Lisa and I stared at each other in disbelief as we started off. We passed people cutting grass and watering flowers in their yards. Just as though nothing had happened. Don't they know Sherry has been killed?

When we arrived at the church, we were stunned to see the crowds of people filing into the sanctuary. Cecil shook his head in wonder. We are a quiet family, and her abundance of friends has always amazed us. She loved so freely. And people responded to her love the same way.

Herman said in his sermon that she left three images of love for us: a beam of light, a flower, and a butterfly. The beam of light symbolized all of the brightness she radiated;

15

the flowers spoke of the love that she planted in our lives and in our hearts which will bloom forever; and the butterfly showed us that she is free from her shell of an earthly body and is alive and more beautiful than ever in heaven. Everyone said the sermon gave them hope, but hope is only for the future. I don't want a future without Sherry.

The children and Cecil and I all held hands when we sang Martin Luther's "A Mighty Fortress Is Our God." It is a hymn of victory, but there is no victory in my little girl being parted from me forever.

I walked out into the night after everyone had gone to bed and sat alone in the swing and tried to pray. Do you think it strange, God, that I can write to you of my anger and my pain, but I cannot bow my head in prayer?

(Sherry, eighteen years ago I gave you life. I held you, rocked you, sang to you, dreamed for you. How could it all be taken away so quickly?)

The sun has disappeared, and the sky is growing dark. Storms usually make me uneasy, but I welcome this one. I must go outside and feel a part of the fury that is blowing lawn chairs over and tearing limbs from trees. The storm can do what I cannot, and I feel almost vindicated as I watch.

My hair and clothes are drenched before I return to the house. Mike and Pat pretend not to notice as I walk by without speaking. I pull my wet clothes off and leave them in a pile on the bedroom carpet. I wish my thoughts were as easy to discard. My mind is so crowded that I don't know which thought to follow. And it doesn't matter because, no matter which one I choose, I lose it somewhere en route.

Yes, I know children die. But, usually, they are sick children or careless children or troubled children. Sherry was none of these. Why, then, is she dead? How could this have happened?

A woman spoke to me yesterday. "I know why my child is still alive and yours is dead," she said. "God knew I was not strong enough to handle something this terrible."

What irony if this is true. Do the weak pray to become strong so they can be brought to their knees and made weak again? The very idea is obscene.

I turn the shower off and know that I can never forgive you, God.

Today is Lisa's birthday. Someone brought her a cake, and we all tried to sit down together and have dinner. A meal without saying, "Sherry is dead." The better part of an hour without crying, "How can we go on?" Instead, we stood like the proverbial wooden Indians singing, "Happy Birthday, Lisa," when we knew it had to be the worst birthday she had ever experienced.

Is there anything more tragic than watching loved ones cover the nakedness of pain with a shallow coating of pretense?

July 10, 1981

Mike and Meredith left to go back to Birmingham today. I am so scared for them to drive that long way home. What if they should have a wreck, too?

We went to the cemetery before they left and stood together among the still lovely floral sprays. I wonder if anyone else felt as detached from the world as I did. I don't think they realize that I have not grasped the realness of Sherry's death. I can say it and I can write it, but I can't "feel" it or believe it truly happened. Death is too permanent for it to come so fast.

The house will soon be empty because all the children will be gone. They have to return to their jobs, and I understand that, but what about my job? I thought it was a full-time commitment helping each child become a Christian adult as well as a productive member of our society. Now my role of mother, teacher, confidante, and friend is ended. Death stole it away. And I am left with the hardest job of all: learning to live with a broken heart.

(Sherry, I *cannot* live without seeing you, touching you. . . .)

It's been a week now since Susie came running up the dusty road to our little mountain retreat to tell Cecil he was wanted on the telephone. A week now, since he walked back into our little house and said in a strained, hoarse voice, "There's been an accident!"

I whirled around from the sink and saw his eyes—shock-glazed and stricken—and knew instantly that one of our children was dead. I stood without moving or breathing, not taking my eyes off his face, and waited for his next words. "It was in Cullowhee . . . ," he began, but stopped when an almost gutteral noise came from my throat instead of the scream it was intended to be.

Seconds later, my body began to shake convulsively and, like an animal faced with sudden danger, my first instinct was to escape. I tore my nightgown off and tried to get dressed, but I was trembling too much to put my hands through the armholes of my bra.

I kept pleading with you, God, and calling out to Sherry while Cecil helped me dress. Even later, when people surrounded me, my lips moved silently and incessantly in prayer. I could not *and would not* accept the horror of what I had heard. To do so would have been a betrayal of faith in the God I trusted.

It was not until Carrol and Ken drove us home and I saw all the cars lined up and down our street that I knew my prayers had been futile. And in that one terrible, earth-shattering moment, everything I had ever believed in came crashing down around me.

Friends were waiting to speak to us, to offer what words of comfort they knew. But I stood mute and wondered why the sun was shining and how my kidneys could still work.

No one seemed to know I was not a part of the world any longer. And no one heard me crying out to my child over and over again in my heart.

People keep coming, and I am weary of being nice. They tell me how strong I am, but I am *not* strong. I am so weak I can hardly make my body go. And the rage I feel over this stupid accident frightens me! Along with the weakness and rage, I am ashamed because of the jealousy I feel when friends come with their children to see us. I know when they leave, they thank you, God, that it is my child and not theirs who has died.

I must be an awful person to have mean and resentful thoughts toward people who are only trying to be kind. It's a paradox because, at the same time, I need the assurance that people care. I do know I feel their sorrow more if they hug or touch me in some way. The jealousy I feel for their untouched families gets in the way, but some love must be seeping through.

I wonder what they would think of me if they could read my thoughts. Does anyone really understand what is going on inside of me? Do they know I am dying, too?

Cecil and I took Pat and Sue to the airport late yesterday. The threat of tears kept our conversation subdued as we walked toward the loading gate. It was hard to say good-bye. I think we have all realized just how fleeting life is.

Since they are resident physicians, I'm sure Mike and Pat deal with death every day, but how different it must be when it involves your own younger sister. I wonder if even seasoned doctors get used to the waste of human lives through an error behind the wheel of a car.

When we returned home, Cecil began cutting the grass, something he always does when he is upset. I opened the door to go inside and, suddenly, my legs just collapsed and I sank to the floor in a first-time-ever, absolutely uncontrollable fit of weeping. Poor Lisa came running, but she felt so unequal to the task of comforting me that she called out to you, God, to tell her what to do. In that instant she could not recognize this distraught stranger as being her mother. But she held me and we rocked back and forth on the floor, the sound of the lawn mower a backdrop for my sobs. We both sensed that for this moment, she was the parent and I the child.

I'm afraid this temporary, but alarming, change in roles made it difficult for her to leave today. She clung to me several minutes before getting into her car to drive away. I hope I was able to assure her that I would be all right. It's hard not to show on the outside how scared I am on the inside.

Can a person ever self-destruct from grief?

I feel so desolate and alone since the children left. Cecil has had to go back to work, even though he comes home several times each day to check on me. My days and nights all run together. I sit and hold Sherry's teddy bear that she has slept with most of her life. And I look at her pictures. Sometimes I cry quietly, but other times I am so consumed with a feeling of sadness and loss that no tears will even come. If the telephone rings or someone knocks on the door, I panic because a decision has to be made, and I simply am not capable of that. So I cover my ears with my hands and wait for the noise to stop.

In the week following the accident, I did exactly what I was told to do. If I was told to eat, I sat down at the table and tried to eat. If someone said I needed to rest, I went to my room and laid down on the bed, obediently closing my eyes. Sometimes I pretended to be asleep when they came to check on me because I could dream of Sherry with no interruptions. I remembered how soft her cheeks were and how bright and merry her eyes were. I even remembered how strong her arms were, whether swimming to win a race, doing gymnastics, or simply hugging me tightly. But, most of all, I remembered her face.

Oh God, what if I forget her face? Please don't ever let me forget her face!

Herman came to see me today and it was good to see him. He has been out of town since shortly after the funeral. I told him we had gone back to church on Sunday although we went late and left early. I felt we could not cope with having to speak to anyone yet. Maybe Cecil could have handled it, but my emotions are not that reliable. I also told him how close I had felt to Sherry in church. Herman didn't think this was strange, but he doesn't know how angry I am at you, God.

He talked with me about some counseling sessions and suggested we meet once a week for several months and talk. He called it working through the grief process and brought me a book to read, called *Good Grief,* by Granger E. Westberg. I don't know how I feel about this. I appreciate his concern, but my feelings are too private to talk about. Besides, it wouldn't change anything. Counseling is not going to make me feel one bit better about Sherry being dead! And I know I wouldn't tell Herman the way I feel inside. I can't let anyone know what a bad mother Sherry had, so the real me has to stay hidden. My life is like a theater play where I recite carefully memorized lines to keep people at a safe distance. It's better for me and better for them, too.

Everyone thinks I am accepting this as just a tragic accident, something that can't be helped, and, with courage, I'll get over it in time. The real truth is that I have no courage. I have been destroyed as a human being and am not living at all. I am merely existing. How could counseling change any of that?

Lying in the dark beside Cecil, it occurred to me if I unpacked Sherry's boxes of clothes that Cecil had so hastily packed on that horrible morning in Cullowhee, I could smell the fragrance of them, and it would be almost like having her here. I jumped up and ran into her room, but when I threw open the boxes, I found that someone had washed and folded everything and put them back all clean and fresh-smelling. I felt as if my heart had been torn apart.

(Oh Sherry, they have even washed the smell of you away. Now I have nothing.)

July 20, 1981

Today was the day for Herman to come, and I was nervous about this so-called grief session. Because he grew up with our boys and loves our family, I am comforted by Herman's presence; and because he is also my pastor, I need the assurance of his faith as well. But to help me accept Sherry's death would be an impossible task for even Herman. It puts a strain on our relationship, and it seems the natural closeness we shared in the past is no longer there.

I listened to him quietly as he talked about his feelings when his father died. Some of the emotions Herman experienced might be like what I am going through, but I don't think anyone can really grasp the enormity of what has happened to Sherry and me. She was a part of me. A part that has been cut away. No one else can feel my pain. My hurt, my thoughts, and even my fears belong to me. I can't share them with anyone.

Before he left, Herman asked if I would like him to pray, and I felt my eyes welling up. I feel a million miles away from you, God, and so desperately alone. While he prayed, I held his hands trying to feel some contact or nearness to you. But when he asked if I wanted to pray, too, I shook my head. There are no prayers inside me. They died with Sherry.

His last words were a gentle reminder that your love for me is stronger than anything I could ever imagine, and it was even now helping to sustain me though I might not realize it. How can this be true? Do you still love me when I doubt, not only your compassion, but even your wisdom? Then why don't I feel your love? I always felt it when I was happy. Now when I really need you, I feel nothing.

Why do some people seem to have a knack for saying the wrong thing to me? Most of my friends are patient, supportive, and loving in just the right way, but a few seem to think they have to give me an answer or a reason for Sherry's accident. And there are none.

I especially hate it when someone tells me how fortunate I am to have all my other children. I wanted all of my children and I love them very much, but right now the resentment over what I don't have gets in the way of being grateful for what I do have. How could I possibly be thankful for the lives of my other children when this same life has been so cruelly snatched away from Sherry?

It has been three weeks since I last saw her, and I have never gone longer than a week in being with her in person or by phone. Herman tells me you are grieving with me, God. You must be weeping with me too then, because that is surely the greatest part of my life. I sometimes think I am going to weep my very life away.

Last night I cried out to Cecil to please help me because I could not bear the anguish another minute. For a moment, his face was contorted with a look of physical pain. Then he cradled me to him and said, "I can't help you because I can't even help myself." We held tightly to each other until, exhausted, we fell asleep.

How long can we go on like this?

Pastor Boye came to sit with us today. We talked about heaven, or at least all that we can know about it from the Scriptures. He said we will recognize each other there even though our bodies will be changed. I think he knew I wanted assurance of that. But I have so many other questions. Why can't I open up more to people?

Cecil began telling him some of the things Sherry's friends have confided to us about our daughter. Her best friend, Beth, told us how Sherry befriended her on her first lonely day at UNCC last fall. Lori remembered Sherry consoling her when she did not make the cheerleading squad. She told Lori God must have something much more important for her to do! Michele spoke of long conversations on the phone. "The bigger the problem, the longer the conversation!" She said, "Sometimes we talked for hours!" Rob, Sherry's steady boyfriend, averted his eyes as he tried to explain why everyone loved her. "She accepted friends for what they were and, somehow, just knowing her made them become better."

Hearing these things makes me proud, but it also makes me angrier! If she could accomplish this much in eighteen short years, just think what she could have done with fifty or so more. I don't understand you, God. You could have saved her, and yet you let it happen. Do you even *care* that my world has crumbled into a million pieces?

When Mike and Meredith called tonight, I could not talk for weeping. Mike kept saying he wished he knew how to help me. But no one can help me. I will never be able to accept what has happened.

My days are a continuing nightmare, and my nights are filled with horror. I dream endlessly of the wreck. A car skids on a rain-slicked highway. A tree looms into view. A crash. A scream. But it is my scream I hear, and it wakes me. I spring to a sitting position, my heart pounding. Cecil tries to hold me, but I cannot stay still. I get up. I pace the floor. I read my Bible, and sometimes I walk outside to look up into the heavens. I wonder where you are, God. I used to feel secure in the nearness of you, but now a torturing question recurs again and again in my mind. Why would the Creator of all life wish harm to come to, not only my daughter, but any innocent child? Is it true, as some lady told me, that you have a plan for every life? Was there some great Master Plan that said Sherry Clark had to die on the fourth of July, and the friend, the rain, the curve in the road, and the tree all just served as agents of this scheme to ensure that she met her destiny?

Then, God, what does this plan offer us when we are standing here with our hearts broken and our world torn apart? Are any goals worthwhile in life, or are they like chances on a raffle that we take in case we live? Are all hopes and dreams meaningless in the end?

Herman came today. He talked of how much I must miss Sherry and how everyone is sharing our sorrow and surrounding us with love. I said I knew that and I appreciated it, but no one could really help us. It had been a bad day, and I was feeling too tired and sad to hide my thoughts.

All of a sudden he said, "I'll bet you're pretty mad at God, aren't you?" I looked up quickly because I didn't think pastors asked questions like that, and I was even more shocked when he added, "I don't blame you! I would be mad, too!" He went on to say that you hadn't wanted Sherry to die, either, God; that you had wanted her to graduate, live a good life, and grow old before coming to be with you.

My eyes blazed a silent question at Herman, and he answered, "But God also wants us to be free to make our own choices, our own decisions. Unfortunately, the choices some people make are very harmful to others. This is when God grieves with us and for us. This is when He understands that we question and grow angry with Him. But God is big enough to take our anger and love us anyway!"

"Do you think Sherry is homesick?" I asked before I had time to think.

"No, I don't," he answered quickly, "because she is at home!"

"But she's not used to heaven," I reminded him, "and she never liked spending even one night away from us. Oh, Herman, I'm just worried about her!" I ended in a low voice, and the tears rolled unheeded down my cheeks.

He took my hand and let me cry for a minute. Then he said, "Martha, the Bible says that God will wipe away every

The Church of Christ 31
Tuscumbia, Alabama

tear from their eyes and also that the heart of man cannot conceive what God has prepared for those who love Him."

I brushed impatiently at my eyes and said, "But what troubles me can't be found in the Bible." And in a rush of words I told him how scared Sherry must have been when she first realized she was dead, wondering what she was supposed to do next, perhaps even weeping within her soul for us and the realization that she was going to be parted from everyone she knew and loved. I could scarcely control my voice as I spoke, and the ever-present tears were falling again.

Herman had tears in his eyes, too, but he quietly began telling me what he believed it was like when Sherry woke up in heaven. He did not deny it might have been a shock to her at first, but he did say he thought the shock was for only a few seconds because the loving arms of our Lord holding her would be enough to calm any pangs of home-sickness or any fears she might have. He also reminded me that time is not a factor in heaven, so she would be more comforted by the fact of our being together for eternity than I am.

I sat quietly for a moment, thinking of what he had said. It did seem to make sense, especially if Jesus stayed close to her.

Herman prayed before he left me, and this time, God, I felt a little closer to you. I wonder why.

Cecil is sick. Last night we were having dinner with Dave and Mimi, and he said he wasn't feeling well. We came home early and I helped him into bed, thinking it was a reaction to stress and depression. During the night, however, he grew much worse, and I had to take him to the hospital emergency room. At first he seemed to respond to treatment, but then he unexpectedly went into shock. Now the doctors tell me he may not live.

Is this some sort of punishment for all my bad thoughts toward you? Are you going to take away everyone I love?

Please, God, take me, too. I cannot bear to have anyone else leave me.

"Go home, dear, and read the Book of Job!" It was an elderly nurse speaking softly to me.

But I don't want to read of anyone else's grief. I have more than enough of my own. For whatever reason Job suffered, God, I have to believe that you did not have a direct hand in Sherry's death or in Cecil's illness.

I remember as a young girl being completely overwhelmed by the strength of Job's faith. I had the noble idea that my own faith would stand the toughest of tests. Today I know I would have buckled at the first tragedy and caused you to be mortified before the powers of evil.

But I do like to read the Psalms, or at least the ones that sound like the psalmist is wringing his hands and screaming out in agony. They fit my mood exactly. I sit for hours pondering the mind of him who wrote them. Dear God, if I had only been there when he sang those songs of pain, the hills would have resounded with my cries and his.

Cecil is still very pale and weak, but the doctors tell me that unless something unforeseen develops, he will recover. He has had a massive blood infection.

The children had all come home again for what we feared was to be another funeral. My mind was so numb that I could not think straight, and the only way I could function was just to move with each moment as it occurred. My thoughts turned inward and I stopped trying to communicate with anyone. You see, God, I felt responsible for Cecil's illness and, if he had died, I didn't know how to explain my guilt to the children. How can I explain things that I don't understand myself? I guess I'm not sure anymore how much our actions count in what happens to us. But I stood quietly grateful when the doctor told me Cecil was out of danger. My mind was amazed over the wonder of events.

Cecil, so sick—but alive. Sherry, so healthy—but dead. What a strange, strange world!

I left the hospital and went to the cemetery to be alone with my thoughts. I know Sherry is not really there, but it helps to go where I can, at least, be near a part of her.

I can scarcely believe so much has happened in only five short weeks. I put my grief aside when I was worried about Cecil, and now that he is better, it has come back again with almost unbearable pain.

> (Sherry, why did you leave me? How can I go on
> without you bouncing into the house and filling it
> with your joy and laughter? Was that really you
> I kissed good-bye on that sad, sad day, or was it
> some lovely wax doll merely like you in its resem-
> blance? Can you understand that my torment
> even includes anger at you for daring to die so
> young and leave me here?)

It all seems like a distant dream. Sometimes I wonder what is real in my life and what is unreal. I say things I must say, do things I must do. But it is not really me. I don't even know who the real me is anymore. Or if there is a real me buried under all this grief.

I think if the world were to open up and drop me into its midst, I could not feel any more powerless over my life. What is the point in planning for a future that is largely out of our control, anyway? Does death always win in the end?

Oh God, today I hurt so. . . .

August 19, 1981

I *laughed* today, God! Not just a polite, meaningless laugh, but a real laugh! Every week since Herman first told me what he believed it was like when Sherry woke up in heaven, I have asked him to tell me about it all over again. And, very patiently, he has always done so. But today, after he repeated his words—the waking, the temporary shock and fright, the reassurance by our Lord that she was safely home, and the loving arms holding her—he suddenly added, "And then Sherry said, 'Lord, please let Mama believe Herman this time!'"

I was shocked out of my reverie, raised my head, and saw the twinkle in his eyes. And, all of a sudden, we both burst into laughter!

The sound of my laughter startled me. It has been so long. I stopped, confused by my feelings. Herman took my hands and said, "It hurts, doesn't it?" When I didn't answer, he added, "You probably feel very disloyal to Sherry, don't you?"

I lowered my head to hide the tears and he went on, "Do you think Sherry would want you to go through life *not laughing?*"

After a long moment of silence, I looked up and whispered, "No, I guess she wouldn't."

And it's true, God. She really wouldn't. Not my Sherry. Not my little sunshine.

It was oddly refreshing to laugh after so many days of pain. But my feelings were mixed with a curious sense of guilt that laughter could chase the pain away, even though it remained hidden somewhere inside waiting to envelop me later.

August 23, 1981

Today Sherry would have been nineteen years old. I hurt in every fiber of my being that I can never celebrate a birthday with her again. It still does not seem real.

Pat and Lisa both came home to be with us for the weekend, and we took Pat's lovely white roses to the cemetery. Herman joined us for dinner after church, and their combined cheerfulness helped lift my depression.

When night came, however, and everyone had gone, I became listless and melancholy again. One minute I wanted to be alone, and the next, I craved companionship. At bedtime I lay down beside Cecil although I knew there could be no rest for me. My mind kept wandering back to this day a year ago.

Sherry was going to move into the dorm at UNCC on the day after her birthday, so we planned a gala celebration to honor both occasions. There was an outdoor cookout with her favorite menu as a surprise.

Mike, Pat, and Lisa sent gifts and also called their little sister on that special day. Brenda, Bob, four-year-old Jennifer, and baby Allison came to the party, arriving early with several gaily wrapped presents. When her friends appeared with even more surprises, Sherry's face showed wonder, elation, and then enthusiastic appreciation for the generosity of everyone. She was always bubbly and effervescent, but on this night she seemed absolutely radiant with the pure joy of being alive, being eighteen, and being so loved! I can see her now with her head thrown back, laughing delightedly at a gag gift she had just opened. Her happiness became a contagious spark for us all.

After dinner, we brought the stereo outside for dancing and lit the tiki torches around the patio. Cecil's eyes grew

38

misty when Sherry put on a waltz record and asked him for the first dance. The flickering light from the torches made her white-clad figure almost fairylike as she waltzed with him, dipping and swaying in the semidarkness. What a magic night it was, God! We all felt it.

It was after midnight when I went into her room to kiss her goodnight and found her reading her Bible. "God is so good to me, Mommy," she said as she looked up. "Sometimes I worry because I have so much."

We talked that night, God, and I learned much about my daughter's faith in you. I also learned about the strength of character she had developed as she tried to live her life the way you would have her to do, especially since her moral values seemed so outdated to her friends. But what I remember most about that night are her starbright eyes when she hugged me and said, "Oh Mommy, I am so excited! It is like I am starting a whole new life tomorrow!"

And college was, indeed, a new life. Living near the dorm made it easy for us to share in the joys and trials of her daily life at school, and we seemed to grow closer even though we were living apart. I was secretly thankful that this last child to leave home had chosen to stay in Charlotte to go to school.

Now it has been another year. And she has begun yet another new life. A life we cannot share. Instead, we are left trying to find comfort in the memories of yesterday.

(Sherry, we thought we had the power to protect you from all harm. But in the end, even our love could not keep you safe.)

Trish came to spend the day with me yesterday. It was so peaceful to go to the cemetery and sit by Sherry's grave with her. We talked about near-death experiences that are occasionally written about and wondered if death is really as peaceful as these people claim. Since Trish is a nurse, she hears much talk about these experiences and remarked to me that no one, having had a deathlike incident, seems to have a fear of dying, even the ones who had been mortally afraid of it in the past.

I found it comforting to sit and talk about death with someone other than one of my pastors. Most people don't like to *think* about death, much less *talk* about it. And my life is just the opposite. Death is the first thing that comes to my mind upon waking and the last conscious thought I have at night.

I sometimes think I am between two worlds. I am alive, but not living. I have experienced death, but I am not dead. I am so lost, God. *Where do I belong?*

Herman and I talked again today. When these grief sessions first began, I didn't want to risk sharing part of my grief with anyone. It almost seemed disloyal to Sherry. Little by little, though, some things are coming out in our talks, and I think it is helping me. Herman knows that I am still angry with you, God, and he prays about it without trying argue with me. He asks me on each visit if I want to pray, too, but I always shake my head, no.

Today he talked about the relationship between parents as they deal with the grief of a child's death. At first, I pretended everything was fine between Cecil and me, but then tears of anger and hurt began to roll down my cheeks as I related how Joan and Aaron had brought dozens of ears of corn to us, and how horrified I was when Cecil immediately began to boil and package the ears for our freezer.

"How could he worry about what we are going to eat next winter?" I wept, saying, "I don't even want to *live* until next winter!"

Herman was quiet for a moment and then he asked, "What did you do while he worked with the corn?"

I told him I had looked at Sherry's pictures and cards and notes that people had sent to me after the accident.

"That helped you a lot, didn't it?" he said. "You were getting help for your grief by engrossing yourself in her pictures and cards and notes."

"Yes, it did help," I agreed.

"But what if you couldn't have borne the pain of looking at her pictures and cards and notes? What would you have done then?"

"I'm not sure," I said, looking up at him as a funny

41

thought occurred to me. "Herman, are you saying Cecil was grieving while he fixed that stupid corn?"

"In his own way, yes," he answered firmly. "For Cecil, cutting the corn, working in the garden, and staying physically busy are some of the ways he is dealing with his sorrow and frustration over Sherry's death."

He went on to tell me that everyone grieves in his own way and on his own timetable and that parents, though they share all other things, can rarely comfort each other over the death of their child.

You know, God, I think he is right. Cecil and I don't share any of the same symptoms in grief. Weeping is an involuntary release for me, and I cannot go over two or three hours without my eyes just suddenly filling up and spilling tears down my cheeks like a summer storm. My stomach cramps in horrible spasms at unexpected moments so that I can never be very far away from a bathroom. I have no appetite, and I rarely sleep for more than a few hours. Even my menstrual periods have become irregular and out of touch with the real me.

But Cecil, though I know he is grieving, never openly talks about his "little girl," as he called her. He is still very pale and weak from his illness, but is so concerned about my weight loss that he cooks breakfast every morning for me so I will eat. At lunchtime, he brings us something special from a restaurant, and after work, he helps me with dinner because I am usually standing in the kitchen wondering what to do first! In other words, he is trying to perform normally, and I have gone from an efficient, creative housewife to some sort of zombie just trying to get through the days.

A few days ago, I was forced to mask my despair and go grocery shopping. I prayed no one would speak to me

because, with my world torn apart, it is hard to communicate with anyone whose world is still intact. I stopped at
Cecil's construction company and, walking into his private
office, I saw him sitting at his desk, his head bowed in grief,
and pictures of Sherry spread out in front of him. I backed
out quickly, my eyes filling with tears. Until that moment,
my hurt had blocked out any thoughts of his pain. He has
held me while I wept and taken care of details when I was
too numb to think. But to break down himself? And why
shut up in his office alone? I knew the answer before I
finished asking the question. He was trying to shoulder my
grief as well as his own. His love for me overshadowed the
natural release of his own suffering. And my pain was so
great that I dared not reach out to him for fear of having
to add some of his hurt to my already bursting heart.

Oh God, I cannot handle what is happening to us. I
would never have believed there was this much anguish in
the world.

Jonnie came over this morning to help me go through some of Sherry's things. She is godmother to all of our children, but was especially close to Sherry. It saddened her heart as much as mine to sort through treasures of eighteen short years.

The cross-stitched pillowcases, the ceramic plaques, and the poetry that were objects of her romantic and creative nature, we put away as keepsakes for her sisters and brothers. The clothes and other useful things were packed up to use or to be given away. The room itself we left as it was with all the posters and teenage bric-a-brac scattered around. No one ever told me how hard it would be to throw a poster away.

When we were almost finished, I was startled to find a copy of a sermon that had been preached by Herman last winter. It must have meant a great deal to Sherry because there were many passages underlined in it. One such passage almost leaped out at me from the paper. It read:

> "Perhaps the only real meaning of darkness is to
> learn the overcoming of it . . . to face the real you,
> the real fears, the real hurts . . . to reach out and
> find the fingers of another touching you in your
> need."

After Jonnie left, I read the words again and again. How could anyone find meaning in suffering like this? And how can I learn the overcoming of darkness when I am blinded by all this pain? Most of my friends expect me to be getting better, and I'd rather pretend than explain. A few do understand and reach out to me but, even when they do, I can't grab hold.

44

I am literally drowning in grief, and there is nothing anyone can do.

I was writing when Herman came for a counseling session today. I closed my notebook quickly, but I think he guessed what I was doing. He just nodded and said it was good to write things down because sometimes that was the only way to get them in the proper perspective. We did not speak of it again.

I wonder why I am almost driven to write down my thoughts. I can always say with a pen what I can't say with my mouth. It's strange, especially since I throw my notes away when everything returns to normal. But now things cannot return to normal because Sherry is never coming back. Days promise nothing but more despair, and writing is the only way I can hang on to the sanity I have left.

(Sherry, my own precious little girl, if I had known how great my suffering would be, I would never have begged God to let me take your place! Your pain, if you had any, was for only a few seconds. I could not bear for you to experience this anguish.)

Today I found Sherry's favorite blouse stuffed into one of her shoe boxes! I was unpacking some of her shoes, and, when I saw it, I thought my heart would stop beating. I buried my face into it, closing my eyes and sniffing the faint fragrance of her body, her cologne, and even her hair spray.

I almost smiled as I pictured her rushing in from class, undressing in a hurry, and stuffing the blouse into this shoe box with full intentions of washing it later. How irritated Lisa and I used to get with her because she never seemed to keep up with those little chores! She was always running from one activity to another, and hiding dirty hand-washables was her unique way of keeping peace until she could find time to do them.

I'm not sure if it helps or hurts to hold something that was close to her body such a short time ago. Perhaps it is not even healthy, but I'm going to put the blouse into a plastic bag and hide it under the bed. Then when the hurt becomes unbearable, I will get it out and smell her and dream.

Why can't I die, too? How long must I live with this terrible pain of knowing Sherry is dead and I am still here? Every chore I try to do takes more effort than I have in my whole body. But I cannot stay still. I pace restlessly through the house and yard. Days are measured only by Cecil's coming and going and by the light which fades into darkness.

Linda walked over this morning to sit with me in the swing. I told her I knew I had to go on living, but I didn't know how to do it. Little Lizzy offered me a broken flower from the garden. Even a toddler knows when someone is sad.

Sensing my depression, Cecil took me to the cemetery, but I became agitated when he suggested watering the straw over Sherry's grave to make the grass begin to grow. I jumped up and ran to the car, upset and not really knowing why. He followed in a few minutes and I reached for his hand to let him know I was sorry. How is it possible to be loved and still feel alone?

Now, at last, relief has come. Your world is asleep, and the flood of tears that have been held back all day is finally unleashed. There are times when nothing else will help but the age-old remedy you provided for pain. Perhaps I can sleep now.

Pat and Sue called tonight and invited us to go to Hawaii with them. They are concerned and want to help by sharing their vacation time with us. I love them for asking us and I love Hawaii, but vacations are for pleasure. And I have no desire for any pleasure now.

I hardly know how to deal with the changes in myself over the past few months. Grieving takes so much of me that it doesn't leave energy for anything else, and it seems to create a need for feeling the pain of denial in my life. To enjoy myself at a party, to play a game of tennis, or even to make love with Cecil would seem wrong with Sherry in the ground. What right have I to have fun or feel pleasure when my child is dead and can feel nothing?

No, God, a vacation would be wasted on me. I don't think I could bear to leave home with all its memories and go away. Besides, when we returned there would just be more changes to face, so why try to run away from our heartache?

Who would have dreamed that the death of a child could have such far-reaching ripples of action and reaction? Grief seems to spiral up and outward until it encroaches upon every aspect of one's world. Nothing is left untouched.

My sorrow has become a yearning for that something in life which will never change.

As summer fades away and signs of fall appear, I cannot believe Sherry has been gone three months. It seems impossible I have even survived three months of knowing she is dead. Sometimes I pretend she is away at college because I like that better than facing the reality of her death. Other times I act almost normal and try to read about and work my way through grief, the way it is deemed best for a grieving mother to do.

Close friends come to sit with me because they know I need their love and support. Other friends are like Job's friends, telling me their personal philosophy of why such a tragedy had to happen.

"You are being tested," one portly woman declared as she sank into the cushions of my sofa yesterday.

"For what?" I queried, "Isn't God omniscient? Doesn't He know me?"

"To see how strong your faith is," she nodded knowingly, "or to teach you something!"

You horrid old woman, I thought to myself. *What makes you think you know the mind of God?* But deep inside I was envious. I wish life and the answers to its puzzling questions were as simple for me to understand.

It must be an awesome responsibility to create a world, God. I wonder what you think as you look upon mankind. What we do seems so out of step with the *why* of our creation. Do you ever weep with us when senseless things happen because of our foolishness?

My heart tells me you do not cause accidents to happen, that they are man-made, not God-made. If I believed otherwise, I could not go on living. I would never accept a God who chose to punish me, teach me a lesson, or make me a

50

better person by taking the life of my child. I can hardly bear the anger of knowing you even *allowed* the accident to happen instead of saving Sherry in some miraculous way, as you could have done. And Job's friends certainly don't help a breaking heart or a wavering faith.

I thought years of careful religious training could withstand any tragedy, but I was wrong. For the first time in my life, I am experiencing serious doubts about my faith. I spend hours searching the Bible for answers to questions I can't even put into words. In Deuteronomy, I find it written in definite terms: "I have set before you life and death, . . . therefore choose life" (30:19). But if one has no faith in the ultimate purpose of existing, why would one choose to live?

And what is faith? How can something so abstract be defined? It is all so confusing, but I must find answers for my questions if I am to have any peace. My thoughts are making me insane.

Another grief session, but this one was different. I talked openly about my notebook and even about the anger and bitterness that is hidden in it. Herman didn't seem surprised and told me that keeping anger all bottled up inside was not healthy, and writing was a good way of letting it out. He said it was also my way of communicating with you, God, and communication of any kind, whether it be anger or gladness, is what prayer is all about.

Of course, I knew my writings were indirectly to you since I always call out to you in my loneliness, but I would not have called it *prayer!* Aren't prayers supposed to be full of thank yous for all our blessings? I know I still have many things to be grateful for, but I can't seem to concentrate on them now. I can only question why you let this horrible accident take Sherry from a life she had not yet begun to live. I am tormented by the fear that she misses me as much as I miss her. That thought is too dreadful to face.

I keep going back to what the Bible teaches us of death and life everlasting. But even Jesus wept over the death of Lazarus. He, of all people, must have known the wonders of heaven. Yet sorrow so filled His heart that it was remembered He wept. And how do we know Mary's innermost thoughts as she watched them crucify her Son? Was the pain she felt any more than mine when I heard Sherry had been killed? Surely, tears shed in grief are the same throughout the ages.

Herman prayed for my faith to make me strong. Did I ever really have faith? It left so quickly, it's hard to know. Am I the only person in the world to question faith and trust and the meaning of life?

52

I never dreamed my body was capable of such a furious exhibition of temper as I displayed today. My nature has been passive, almost docile, since July, and I thought I wasn't capable of showing emotion anymore. To express emotion takes energy, and I am too lethargic nowadays for that. Nonetheless, something must have built up inside me until I could no longer contain it while reading that magazine today. I am still aghast over what happened.

It had been a quiet morning and a not too unpleasant one. Carol was over for coffee, and we talked about Sherry and her Janet when they were toddlers together. And, God, I so desperately need talks about Sherry's life! It helps put the pieces of me back together again to remember things that were good. I know I can't live forever in the past, but right now it is essential for me to retrace and savor precious moments.

After lunch, I was lonely and glad to see the postman come with our mail. I read several cards and notes and then opened a thick envelope with an out-of-town postmark. It was from an old friend who had sent me a copy of a monthly religious magazine she receives. Out of curiosity, I immediately sat down on the sofa to read it.

As I turned the pages of this little booklet, I read of one miracle after another where, always at the last minute, you stepped in and saved the author's spouse, child, relative, or the author himself from certain death or tragedy. Each story was a proclamation to the readers about your glory because of this miracle and a statement of how radically changed the author's life had thereby become.

I was breathing hard—so hard my chest hurt—and my eyes were swimming in tears when, suddenly, I lost control

53

and hurled the magazine through the living room and into the dining room. I watched it sail over the table and strike the mirror before it fell to the floor.

I was almost incoherent as I burst out from the depths of my soul that I could have written a story telling readers of your glory, too, if I had received a miracle! I could have told people of your great love for mankind, too, *if I had received a miracle!* And I would have told the *world* how my life had been changed, *IF I HAD ONLY RECEIVED A MIRACLE ON THAT AWFUL NIGHT IN JULY!* I demanded to know who was in charge of handing out miracles, and why wasn't I chosen to have received one? I hardly recognized the loud, angry voice I heard as being mine.

Exhaustion finally took its toll, and I collapsed on the sofa in sobs. But my cries faded when I began to sense an erie quality somewhere in the room. As strange as it may seem, I had a feeling you were there, God. I even thought I felt the pressure of your hand on my head. I was frightened, but I didn't want to move. I don't think I *could* have moved! Then a dreamlike calm took possession of my body, and thoughts moved across my mind like a television camera focused on a slow-moving parade.

I was mesmerized as I relived all the miracles you have performed for me during my lifetime. I saw Sherry as a toddler, choking in that department store, with me working frantically to get a piece of candy out of her throat. She had turned blue before I was able, in some inexplicable way, to dislodge it with my finger digging into her throat. When she gasped her first lifesaving breath, I hugged her, never wanting to let go, and thanked you for the miracle that I knew had taken place. How could I ever forget that day?

The picture changed to show me Lisa and Sherry, standing beside a plastic wading pool in our backyard, angrily

54

tugging on a sopping wet beach towel. Suddenly, a bolt of lightning snaked down from the sky and struck a tree in the next yard, sending shock waves out with an earsplitting boom echoing all around us. To my horror, I saw both little girls tossed into the air before landing on their backs in the grass. I ran to them, begging you to save their lives. And you did, because when I reached them, I found they were breathless, stunned, and frightened, but not hurt in any way.

I was forced to remember other miracles, too, involving all the children as well as Cecil and me. Some miracles I remembered and others I didn't, but all were shown as being part of my life from childhood until now. There was no doubt in my mind that the miracles I couldn't recall actually happened. I don't know why I was so positive of this, except that it was all there. As though I were watching a film of my entire life.

At the end of this strange scenario, I was too drained to move, but my brain was whirling. I was astonished that you chose to speak to me when I was so angry! How could you know I would even listen? Or were you waiting for just such a moment to show me how close you are, and always have been, to me?

For the first time, I am beginning to understand how committed your love is to me, and without asking anything in return. Not even my loyalty or the ability to thank you for the things I still have.

I think it is true. You really have been weeping with me all through my sorrow. But not just for my loss of Sherry. You were also weeping for your loss of me.

How many years I have taken the church for granted! I dismissed as clichés all the words used to describe its people. The priesthood of believers and the body of Christ were mere jargon until they suddenly became the parts of me that could not think or feel.

Sunday after Sunday, they sing hymns I have no strength to sing, pray prayers I have no faith to pray, and profess a belief in something I no longer understand. It fuses us together even though we are aeons apart. And hearing the familiar and ancient liturgy calms and comforts me as nothing else can.

Sometimes I weep when the processional starts because it is beautiful and Sherry loved it so. "It's like we're marching into heaven!" she would whisper when we rose for the first hymn. Her eyes would shine as she sang the hymns and prayed the prayers that were so much a part of her life in this church. Now she is somewhere else, and she sings hymns and prays prayers we have yet to learn.

For too many of us, I am afraid religion is rather benign. It is easy to make emotional commitments, sing hymns of praise, and promise everything to you. But when something happens to destroy our world, we find faith hard to live. And the more we try to hang on to faith, the more elusive it becomes. Yet the church stays the same, and the sense of continuity it gives us never seems to waver or to end.

I can't help but think this is why, even though I feel dead inside, I am surviving.

The nights are still hard. I am restless and can sleep for only short periods. My mind goes over and over the last nineteen years, taking out and examining even the smallest memory. I am so afraid I will forget something and it will vanish, never to be recalled again.

In today's early dawn, I remembered Sherry coming to me one day when she was only four years old. Her siblings had refused to let her join their game of Monopoly, and her little heart was broken.

"I wish I was all growed up!" she sobbed, rubbing her eyes in anger and frustration.

I stooped down to hug her, even then realizing that day would come far too soon for me. But her time for being "all growed up" never came, God, and it hurts to see the world go on as if her life were too fleeting to have mattered at all.

I said this to Herman today and, without thinking, blurted out that all I had left were her blouse and the smell of her body to convince me she ever lived at all.

His astonishment was not feigned. "Nothing left but her blouse and the smell of her body?" he asked, shaking his head in disbelief. "The love she shared, the lives she touched, the flowers she planted in our hearts? Those are things that live forever! But as long as you depend on the fragrance of a blouse to remind you of her, you won't ever be able to appreciate the real and important things she left!" He looked at me with a gentle, but incredulous, expression.

I was crushed. How could he fail to understand? I was living with grief and bereaved love, and I *needed* to hold onto something concrete when I dreamed of Sherry.

While I was struggling for words, Herman spoke again.

57

"The scent of her blouse will fade in time," he said, " and you'll see it was never really a part of Sherry at all. But the love she shared reaches far beyond death, and that will never die!"

I turned away from his emphatic words. Nowadays, any absoluteness in someone's manner makes me uneasy, for I doubt even the most simple decisions. He came quickly, then, and hugged me.

"I loved her, too, you know," he said quietly.

And I do know. But there seemed nothing more to say.

Vacation or escape? The question wouldn't go away as we boarded the plane for Hawaii. I could scarcely believe it was me buying tickets, packing bags, and making arrangements to meet Pat and Sue in Chicago.

I did not try to leave my grief behind, for it would have meant leaving Sherry behind, too. So here I am with the devastation of fresh grief turned into an ache that never completely goes away. It's not better, just different.

Walking into the terminal in Chicago, we could see Pat and Sue searching the incoming passengers for us. They looked excited, but anxious. My heart overflowed with love for them as they saw us and waved. For the first time in months, I began to relax a little bit. There was even a tiny glimmer of being glad I came.

> (Do you understand, Sherry? Can you see that I
> have to get away and look for the parts of me that
> are lost? It doesn't have anything to do with my
> love for you. Or my wanting you. That will never
> change. But I have given your family so little
> lately that sometimes I weep over that, too.)

Soft Hawaiian music greeted us when we entered the big 747 which was to take us to Honolulu. We were shown to our seats by attendants wearing gaily flowered shirts and muumuus. The spaciousness of the plane fascinated Pat and Sue, and we were amused over their childlike delight. The pilot maneuvered the plane into position for takeoff, and we climbed skyward over a cold and beautiful Chicago.

The passengers were quiet and seemingly lost in thought as we passed over cities in Illinois, small towns in Iowa, and checkerboard farms in Nebraska. It was five hours later, and we had been flying over the Pacific Ocean for about an hour when I realized what a long day it had been. And how weary I was.

Reaching for my pillow, I stretched out on the seat beside me to rest. I closed my eyes and listened to the drone of the huge engines, marveling over the tremendous technological advances of the human race. How far we have come, God! And yet everything we experience has a mirrored edge to it. This plane that is taking us across the Pacific is causing too much pollution for our world. Those beautiful, tropical islands we are going to visit were formed by violent eruptions of lava spewed forth by ancient volcanoes.

The same mirrored premise can be said for mankind. Joy and sadness are intermingled in our lives: pain and good health, the high times and the valleys, human knowledge mirrored with a thirst for power. What we can do is so much more than what we are. It is a sobering thought. What pushes us onward? Is it faith? I found my questions disturbing.

Suddenly, my eyes flew open as the thought exploded in my mind that faith is *everywhere!* It never gets lost, even though we might. Decisions are made every day based on faith, whether we realize it or not. By faith, we bought our airline tickets; by faith, we climbed on board; and, by faith in intricate radar systems at the airport, our pilot will land this plane in the darkness on a small island in the middle of the ocean.

Then faith cannot be some innate quality that a person automatically has with no effort on his part. It doesn't just *happen.* We *choose* to have faith by looking at a situation and making a decision. This mysterious faith, that we can't see or feel, is an innermost part of our lives. And faith in God must be the same. To believe in Him as Creator means to take the evidence of our world and make a choice. To believe that Jesus Christ was born, lived, was crucified, and rose again means to take the evidence of eyewitnesses and make a choice. And, once decided, this very act becomes a commitment to what we believe: a living faith that helps us weather the storms of life.

I smiled as I realized my faith didn't die when Sherry died. I only thought it did because I couldn't feel your presence. But a faith dependent on feelings is not really faith at all, is it? Calling out to you when I *couldn't* feel your nearness was faith in the truest sense—the kind of faith that counts.

How special to learn that up here in the air, so close to you!

Dear God, I had forgotten how beautiful your world is. We retrace steps we took with Sherry, Lisa, and David three years ago. I point out the inlet where Sherry learned to surfboard. Cecil and I laugh at the memory of her many splashes into the water before she learned to ride the towering waves.

Sue and I walk around the lagoon watching children play in the sand. People smile at you here, completely uninhibited and never doubting that you will smile back. No feelings, no intimacies will be exchanged. You are free to wear your mask just as they wear theirs.

At night we settle back on our balcony and look at the stars over the skyline of Honolulu. How small we are under the vastness of the universe! The minutes pass with few words spoken, but there is closeness and love in the silence of our thoughts. And a sense of peace.

Sundays are special days, and I was worried about being so far away from our church and the people I love. Sometimes I forget, God, that it is your presence uniting the worshipers in church, not the church itself, that gives me strength to make it through the week.

Cecil and I read in Ecclesiastes this morning, and, as usual, I became totally absorbed in its wisdom. It seems to say so much more than I can comprehend. Is it true that every season will have its happiness as well as its misery? Does this mean that happiness can come again to those of us who are suffering if we but let it? And since we forget former happiness so easily in times of grief, is it also possible that someday we might forget today's misery as well?

It makes me wonder if Jesus Himself went through all the stages of happiness and grief to show us that His life was no less and no more than the story of humankind. The thought is comforting on this sabbath.

We worshiped in what is known as the "Penthouse" Lutheran Church in downtown Honolulu. It was beautiful and awesome to see the panoramic view of the island and listen to the pastor speak at the same time. Hawaiians sing hymns in a lower and more melodious tone than we do on the mainland. But the service is the same, and the rootedness of our faith is what I needed.

Five thousand miles from home, God, and your people are the same. Maybe it *is* impossible for one to ever be homesick in heaven.

How fast these days have passed. Now we are on the way home and will spend the last of our vacation time in San Francisco. A storm has hit the city unlike any since the early part of the century, but we went sight-seeing, anyway.

Sue and I screamed when Cecil drove down the famous crooked road. We admired the old houses and talked about the people hurrying about in the rain. An old lady carried a water-soaked bag of groceries, and I wondered aloud if she lived alone and how far she had to go. Pat smiled and questioned why a young boy on a bicycle was out in the rain and not in school. We mused over the natural curiosity of humans and decided it was more good than bad.

In Chinatown, we left the car and sloshed our way from one shop to another. How ancient and mysterious everything looked! The exquisite articles of beauty span both cultural and language barriers. There was a coziness among strangers as we shopped.

The waterfront was ominous and gray, but still bustling with people. Umbrellas turned inside out with the wind and were soon discarded. Like children, we jumped over the biggest and deepest puddles, laughing when a misplanted step sent cascades of water out in every direction.

We arrived at a restaurant, and the aroma of delicious food made us forget our soggy appearance and fatigue. Our talk was animated and cheerful. A perfect ending to an extraordinary day of sight-seeing.

Exhaustion had set in by the time I showered and climbed into bed beside Cecil. He moved his newspaper to make room for me, and I snuggled close to him. I was sinking into that stage between consciousness and sleep when a write-up of a head-on collision caught my eye.

64

Suddenly wide awake, I saw that two teenagers had died in the fiery crash. Dear God, will it never stop? I closed my eyes to shut out the horror, but it was too late. The pain defeated me, and I began to weep for those parents who, too quickly, became people of sorrows and acquainted with grief.

With questions unasked and unanswered, Cecil held me through the night.

Beth had a big welcome poster up when we returned home tonight. How like Sherry she is! The resemblance is almost startling with her dark curls and dancing eyes, and even their personalities are the same. She was a part of our daughter's life. A living part that comforts us by her love and concern.

Oh God, I dreaded coming back to this house knowing Sherry wouldn't be here, but I knew I couldn't run forever. The holidays are coming, and they must be faced.

How will I stand it? Trying to picture Thanksgiving without Sherry making the stuffing for the turkey or Christmas without her decorating the tree is impossible. How can I hang up the stockings and leave her hook on the fireplace empty?

There will be heartaches for all of us. What will Lisa do without Sherry to giggle with as they wrap presents? How will Pat buy his gifts without Sherry accompanying him as she has always done? Who will make Mike the butterfinger cookies he loves? How can we sing the carols in church without her sweet voice beside us? I am going crazy asking myself questions, but I can't seem to stop.

I thought when my faith returned, it would push the anger and longing for her out of my brain. But here I am . . . still angry, still hurting, still weeping.

Will I ever get used to the unsettled feelings of the new me?

My mornings are a study in contrast. Sometimes I wake and have no memory of my grief. For one moment, I am completely happy. Then, from somewhere deep inside, what has happened creeps into my consciousness, and sadness overwhelms me. I want to close my eyes and shut out the world.

Other mornings I wake and know that I have dreamed of Sherry. I lie still and revel in the joy of knowing we have been together again. Dreams are like teardrops, soothing us after some great hurt to our body or spirit. A catharsis of the mind. Probably a unique gift.

The contradictions of life are hard to explain and harder to accept. I thought Sherry's future belonged to her and to us when it really didn't. That was my mistake, and I cannot come to terms with it. I loved her so much, and I wanted to keep on loving her, but suddenly she was gone. And with her went all the things she might have been.

Dear God, I think it will take the rest of my life to learn to live with things as they are, rather than as I believed they would be.

I always cherished the holiday traditions that were a part of my heritage. I wanted to make them a part of my children's memories, too. It was a special time to plan and make decorations, as well as a time to share with each other the joy of belonging. But when this day of Thanksgiving arrived, I was forced to combine the colorful traditions of a lifetime with the pale fragility of life itself. The dilemma seemed to match my ambiguous thoughts.

I wanted and needed to go to church, but the first hymn was "Now Thank We All Our God," and I could not sing the words. It was good to have the children home with us, but their presence made me sense Sherry's absence more than ever. I prepared all the old favorites for our dinner, but they were hardly touched even though everyone kept saying how good the food was. Before we sat down to eat, Pat prayed that we might live according to your will so that our family would one day be united again in heaven, but my heart froze in fear that my doubts would keep me from ever going to heaven at all. Each part of the day has been governed by a memory, and I seemed powerless to change the pattern.

One by one, Cecil and the children had gone to Sherry's grave for a few quiet moments. I had been busy with dinner, but soon my work was finished, and the day stretched endless before me. I was more restless than tired, but deeply troubled that the day had been so sad. When Herman dropped by and asked me to visit the cemetery with him, I quickly accepted. I wasn't sure whether it was to escape the strain of pretending this was a normal Thanksgiving or whether I needed to be at the site of my last moment with

Sherry. But for either reason, I felt a sense of relief to put on my raincoat and leave the house.

By the time we arrived at the cemetery, a light fog was rolling in, and my mood was as gray as the day. I was startled when Herman suggested I begin the prayer this time and had to take a deep breath to cover up my fright. Not once since Sherry's death had I offered up a real prayer! Yet suddenly I *wanted* to pray. My mind was a jumble of confusion as we knelt on the damp ground. How was it possible to give thanks for the things I have learned without denying the bitter feelings I still have over my loss? The world was silent while I searched for words to explain my heart.

After a long moment and in a voice almost too low to be heard by human ears, I confessed that I still hate what has happened. I even hate learning that faith doesn't take away the hate. This strangest of all prayers, so long denied, was filled with all the loneliness, heartache, and doubts that I have felt since Sherry's death.

But the longer I prayed, the more relaxed I became. It was as though a large key was unwinding me, and the tautness was leaving, little by little. And then I thanked you, God, for the love and support that have been shown to us by so many people. People who had faith, not only in you, but also in us. People who proved that faith, so hard to define and yet so much a part of life, would help me see beyond the hate and hurt of the present. And, in a gesture of simple trust in that faith, I asked your help in learning to live again.

For a moment, I couldn't believe I had said the words! Me wanting to live again? My life had become one of confusion, and the me I remembered had disappeared months ago. Could I actually be asking for help? Shocked,

69

I raised my head and stared at Herman. Without a word, he finished the prayer. But I can recall nothing he said.

I felt strangely calm when we returned home and tried harder to make the rest of the day pleasant for everyone. When friends of Sherry's came by that night, I was genuinely pleased to see them. We talked about her in a loving, gentle way that made me feel warm and good inside. For the first time, God, I realized they have suffered a great loss, too.

What a long, long time it has taken me to notice.

Pious platitudes and biblical explanations have never done anything to help my sorrow. I secretly think such talk is easy as long as the death you are trying to explain is in someone else's family.

"She's not gone. She's just away," a friend consoles me. But she *is* gone. In fact, she is *dead.* D-E-A-D. A word that will make the strongest person cringe. A word everyone tries to hide from. The mirror edge of life itself.

"Her work on earth is finished, so God took her home," an elderly lady assured me the day of the accident. Yes, her work is finished, but only because of a tragic accident that crushed the beginning of a beautiful and promising life. I know you welcomed her home, God, but I cannot believe you gave her precisely eighteen years and ten months to live and, when that time was up, you saw that she climbed into a car and then sent it crashing into a tree.

My view of you is not so harsh now, although there were times when I wanted to blame you. But I have come to realize there will always be unfathomable mysteries about life. We may never know why one child gets a new bicycle and another one gets leukemia. Or why one person escapes a car accident without a scratch and another one dies. Or even why there is so much sadness in some lives and almost none in others. But we do know that you loved us enough to take on human flesh and share the same pain and sorrow of the world through your Son.

It helps me to remember how committed Sherry was to a belief in this Jesus Christ. A friend of hers had been killed in an accident and, in spite of her shock at death intruding into her private world, she did the things she had to do. After the funeral, I saw her sitting quietly in her room.

Thinking she was just sad, I stopped to give her a hug. But she turned around and I saw the tears. "Oh, Mommy," she said with a heartbroken sob, "If I could only be sure he was a Christian, I wouldn't worry."

And, God, even though I cannot thank you for Sherry's life without giving a thousand reasons why she should still be with us, I can be grateful we don't have that worry. I am confident she is with you. Even in my worst moments, that thought will not be denied.

Life inches slowly toward the holiday season, and my emotions vary from day to day. For the most part, I'm into a routine and can handle my household duties again. But any deviation from that routine brings instant tears and feelings of distress.

Thoughts of decorating the house and shopping for gifts make me panic. I don't think I could handle treating this Christmas as any normal one. Yet how sad for Cecil and the children to think that not even they are enough to make me forget my grief.

Life is not easy, God, and things look different from where I am. Suffering goes on all over the world, and we are only vaguely aware of it. But when tragedy strikes us, it sharpens our senses and we begin to notice suffering in the lives of others. After a while, one can't help but wonder why a world so full of pain was created. How ludicrous it seems to lay aside the hurt and try to rejoice in anything, even the coming of the Christ Child. It is surely a tribute to the tenacity of mankind that they have been doing this for so many years.

I love you, God, and I love my family, too. But I think I will sit this one out. It will be safer to watch Christmas as a spectator than to risk getting involved.

Why do we build invisible doors around us when we are hurting? Is it because we don't want anyone to come into our world and see what pain has done to our lives? Most of the time people are rebuffed by these doors, but Christmas seems to bring with it a time for reaching out, a need for sharing with those who suffer. We see this now in special gifts of love from our friends.

Diana and Tami dropped by with a casserole for our dinner, and Geri made us some of her special cookies. Jonnie and Leslie brought over a large basket of fruit and wanted to know if there was anything they could do for us. Carrol calls nearly every day from her home in Spindale, and even Ann picked up baby Kristin from the nursery and surprised us with a visit on her way home from work. We are more touched than they know. Without friends, this season would be unbearable.

Perhaps it is not important to worry whether Christmas has become too commercialized as long as we remember to give the most important gift of all . . . that of ourselves.

Look at me, God! It's Christmas Eve, and I have a tree, a wreath, some wrapped gifts, and even a turkey thawing in the refrigerator.

I'm not sure when I began to change my mind about Christmas. At first I avoided all mention of the word, and no one dared bring it to my attention. But friends began to drop by, there were more hugs and warm handshakes from people at church, and even the clerks in stores seemed more helpful than usual. I sensed, not just a vague holiday spirit in the air, but a real awareness of love reflected in the sentimentality of the season.

From earliest childhood, we are taught that the first gift of Christmas was God Himself. By taking on human flesh and dwelling among us in the physical world, Jesus became one with us, the living proof of your love and a promise of life to come. And this incredible gift meant that, by choice, you became a bereaved parent, too!

My mind marvels as I reflect on the paradox involved here. From the moment of His birth, you knew the story of His life. And of His death. Dear God, you must have grieved even as you rejoiced when the angels sang hosannas on that first Christmas day. Perhaps it is in recognizing this that my heart can ache for the sorrows of the world and still find joy in the celebration of your love in person.

I once thought it was a miracle that, even in the darkness, the shepherds found the Babe of Bethlehem. Tonight I don't find it miraculous at all, because in another kind of darkness, these many years later, I think I have found Him, too.

No one was more surprised than I when this Christmas, sadder than any I had ever known, still had meaning and was rich in spirit. Perhaps the unity of sorrow we shared helped to make it so.

Most of my thoughts are fleeting, and I cannot hold on to them for long. But during the holiday season, they were orderly and not as fragmented. There was no flash of sudden insight or miracle of answered questions. Just the steady and growing influence of people who shared what we could not find by ourselves.

Although I knew we would have to buy a few gifts, I was determined not to decorate the house or even to have a tree. I confided this to Herman one day. He nodded and said, "I don't think you should have a tree." And I was glad he agreed with me. But then he added, "If the only reason you ever had a tree was because of Sherry!" It made me ashamed of the person I had become.

The next afternoon I found myself at a Christmas tree lot walking through rows of different trees. I shivered in the cold. A young boy came to help me, stuffing mittenless hands into his pockets. But I didn't know which tree to choose. There were too many. The familiar feeling of helplessness was taking over, and I started to leave before the tears came.

I stopped in front of a small, spindly tree at the edge of the lot. It was tied to a stand and leaning sideways, almost to the ground. *That tree is like me,* I decided. *It's not even able to stand upright without help.* "I'll take that one," I said quickly and lowered my head, pretending to be busy getting money out of my purse.

"You'll have to cut the limbs off the bottom to make it

fit into a tree stand," the boy explained. "And if you nail 'em back into the trunk of the tree, it'll shape up real nice." He carried it to the car for me and, wishing me a merry Christmas, hurried back to the fire.

Cecil made no comment when he lifted it out of the car, and I offered no excuses for the ugly little tree. After dinner, he brought it into the house and, with the bottom branches sawed off, the tree looked worse than ever. But, remembering what the boy had said, I went outside and gathered up the excess greenery. I placed one feathery branch at the bottom of the tree and asked Cecil to nail it in. And, with few words passing between us, we began tacking and twisting other branches into place.

To our astonishment, the tree began to take on real beauty and shapeliness. Standing back, we admired our handiwork and smiled at each other. We had made something beautiful out of something ugly. It was a good feeling.

The closeness between us continued in a midnight talk. I confessed that I had seen a painful reminder of myself in that frail little tree. And I wondered if it was also a symbol of the missing parts of me that were being repaired with extra branches, or shoots of love, from others.

It was a special night, God. And somehow I wasn't surprised to feel a desire to become Cecil's physical wife again. A most fitting occasion for love to happen.

A new year, and the world goes on. Never again can we say, "This year Sherry was killed." Now it will have to be, "Last year . . . ," and someday it will even be, "Five years ago . . . !" We are leaving her behind and, for me, it is like trying to walk away from my shadow.

Meredith and Mike came to spend a few days with us, and we invited friends in to see the old year out. It was my first attempt at entertaining since Sherry's death, and the whole idea was rather frightening. No one would ever admit it, but friends are not as comfortable with us as they used to be, and knowing this makes us uneasy, too.

I was grateful that Meredith assumed the role of hostess whenever I faltered. Smiling, talking, and passing hors d'oeuvres are duties I used to perform with no effort. Now each task needs all my concentration, and I can handle only one chore at a time.

But perhaps I expect too much. Sitting in the cluttered aftermath of party-making, I wonder if a certain lightheartedness will not always be missing from our lives now. No matter how good things might be in years to come, there will always be the awareness that we have experienced life's greatest tragedy—an anguished reversal of the natural order of death.

Can the zest for living, that natural spontaneity of life itself, ever come back in the face of such knowledge?

For the last six months, my mind has been filled with as many ups and downs as a roller coaster ride. Doubt, anger, and depression have all fought for control of my life. It was a whirling existence and the spin has left me breathless and exhausted. I wanted to slow things down, sort things out, but I didn't know how to do it. Or even if I had the strength to try. I only knew that, for the first time, a strange and fearsome quality of having no control over our destiny had been introduced into my life.

It was easy to concentrate on the simplicity of life when I was younger and my world was small! Now I am older and the more I know, the less I understand. Some days my mind won't stop as I struggle over what I cannot solve.

There are a million "ifs" in my thoughts today. If we hadn't let Sherry go to summer school. If we had fixed her old car up so she could have taken it to Cullowhee. If we had insisted she spend that last weekend with Lisa as she had originally planned. If, if, if . . . ! There must have been a thousand ways to prevent her death, but we had no way of knowing, and she died.

Life is filled with so many deceptive events, choices that seem right, but turn out wrong. Do our decisions alone cause heartache, or are you the author of tragedy and sorrow? Is bad considered good if you do it? Do we live in any kind of a predictable world at all? It seems reasonable to believe that life makes sense, but sometimes it doesn't.

My doubts are so strong today, they overshadow any faith I thought I had. The sense of direction I was beginning to regain is all blurred, and I see the future with a big hole in its center. Why has this depression come again? Why is my life suddenly penetrated with great bursts of wanting

79

Sherry after six months of slowly getting better? Was the peace I felt during Christmas only a false high that was bound to end after the holidays? Or is grief ever so simple that one can say with finality that it is over?

What is happening to me? Every night before sleep comes, my life flashes before me. Or at least that longest part of my life, the last six months. Each terrible moment is permanently engraved upon my brain, and I must lie helpless and view each detail in its entirety before exhaustion finally brings relief.

I feel again the horror of Cecil's telling me what had happened to Sherry. I see the pity and compassion on Susie's face. I remember listening to my brother, Bob, on the telephone and looking up only a few hours later to see him walk into the mountain house. I knew, even in the chill of shock, that he must have left Augusta within minutes to get there so fast.

I agonized because no one knew where Lisa was and worried when I heard Mike and Meredith had left Birmingham so quickly for the long drive home. Once more I hear Pat's voice as he called from the airport in Gainesville and again from the airport in Atlanta when he and Sue changed planes there.

My stomach tightens into a knot when I remember dialing and dialing and not being able to reach Herman. I sense loved ones filtering into the house as they heard the news, all wanting to do something when there was nothing they could do.

I can hear Ken talking in his calm and steady voice on the drive back to Charlotte and feel the fan blowing cold air on my face. My head ached, but the pain was bearable because I thought small pains might keep me from thinking about bigger ones. I remember going into the rest room at a service station and blurting out to some young girl in a leather jacket, "Sherry's been killed!" Then I turned from her startled eyes and ran back to the safety of the car. I laid my head on Carrol's shoulder and sobbed because I had put the nightmare into words for the first time.

My friend Joan opened the car door when we stopped in the driveway, and Herman walked me to the house. I had no idea what I was saying to him then, but I remember the words now. I looked at and did not see friends then, but I can see them now. I can even see what they were wearing.

And through that first anguished day, I prayed and prayed that Sherry was not dead. Not my Sherry. Let it be a mistake, I begged. But it was true and, even as I fought it, I knew. Sherry was gone, and there was nothing anyone could do to help me. This kind of suffering had to be borne alone.

The ground is covered with a thick blanket of snow. No one can come for a visit, and even the telephone does not work. Once I would have welcomed a reprieve from life's demands, but now it buries me as easily as it does the crocus peeking up in our garden.

I hear children laughing outside, and memories of Sherry and her friend William sledding in last year's snow are roused in my mind. When will this stop? I think I am going insane. But pain won't be reasoned with, and I close my eyes. If I hold my thoughts together, God, I can pretend she is only away at school.

(Sherry, you asked me not to get tears in my eyes that last time we said good-bye. You hugged me and said you wanted to remember me with a smile on my face forever. So I smiled as I waved, never dreaming that in only a matter of days, my smile would disintegrate into a frozen mask of anguish. And that the memory of you—the way you looked and the things you said—would have to last for a lifetime. I wonder if anyone ever realizes what they have when they have it.)

"I'm getting worse instead of better," I announced to Herman today. "My nights are spent reliving every horrible detail of Sherry's accident, and my days are filled with pretending it never happened at all! Her death day is like an obsession with me, and I can't put it out of my mind."

I bent my head to hide the tears and added, "I don't think counseling will ever work for me. I only want my daughter back, and nothing is ever going to change that."

For a few minutes, there was only the sound of the clock ticking in the room. Then Herman said, "You know, Martha, I see positive things beginning to happen through these thoughts, even though they seem sad. Perhaps you haven't been ready to pick up and examine these hurtful details until now."

I didn't answer, and he kept on talking, "Remember the nightmares of the wreck you used to have when the crash of the car would wake you up? You thought those would never stop, but they did. And remember how you pulled up blades of new grass from over Sherry's grave to keep it from looking permanent? But the grass grew faster than you could pull it up and, in the end, you had to accept it. Then we were able to *use* the grass as a soft cushion for us to sit on, stand on, and even kneel on while we were there."

I had raised my head to listen and broke in, "I know some things are better, but this depression is different!"

But Herman teasingly held his hand up to indicate he wasn't through talking and continued, "The first words you said to me when you got out of the car that afternoon were 'Herman, I never want to hear laughter again!' But, Martha, you did laugh. And, even though you felt so guilty

84

about it that you cried, it was a first step. Wouldn't you admit you've taken a lot of first steps since then?"

"You mean, like Christmas?" I was puzzling over his words.

He nodded. "It would have been abnormal for you not to grieve over Sherry's absence on such a special holiday. But, by going ahead with the same traditions your family had always observed, you firmed up the shaky ground you were standing on and helped everyone else, too."

"What about the pretending?" I asked, expecting a negative reply.

And Herman surprised me by saying to pretend is not bad as long as you remain in charge of it. He suggested I pretend Sherry was in the room with me and not away at school, as I usually did. "Have a definite time for the beginning and the end of the visit," he said. "That way, you will be in control of the fantasy instead of having it control you."

I pondered his words silently. It would certainly be no problem to pretend. My only problem nowadays was in trying to live *without* pretending!

How could the thing I do best suddenly become impossible to do? Even though I tried, I could not pretend Sherry into existence for a visit. It's one thing to imagine her away at college and quite another to pretend she is here. Grief has propelled me into a state of limbo where I neither accept her death nor believe in her presence. Yet I see the benefits of such a fantasy. There are many things I could say to her that no one else would understand. Unfortunately, knowing something is good doesn't guarantee being able to do it.

Perhaps the only way to overcome this obstacle is to have an imaginary visit on paper. Writing has shaped most of my dreams. Why could it not pretend a dream as well?

Would it be permissible, God, for me to write one of your angels a letter?

MY DEAREST SHERRY,

Herman suggested I pretend you are here, instead of away at school as I usually do. So I am picturing you all curled up in your daddy's chair with your legs thrown over the side and your head back. Your favorite place in the house to rest, watch TV, or just sit and talk. And I will write my words to you. That way I won't have to look up and see you are really not here at all.

Are you truly happier where you are? Can the joys of this mysterious heaven be enough to make you feel as loved and secure as you were in your earthly life? My faith has wavered so much in the past months. Only once in a very great while do I find myself being glad you are home. Home, as I could never make it, and safe, as I could never make you totally safe. No, darling, I'm afraid most of my days have been despairing ones, and I felt both abandoned and betrayed by God as I tried to comprehend what had happened to us. You in heaven and me on earth? What madness was this? We belonged together until you married or moved out!

I could not absorb the words when I heard you were dead. My mind refused to believe that my merry, joyous Sherry, the light of my life, was gone.

When I finally reached Herman on the telephone, I could not speak, other than to say my name. I wanted to ask him, because I couldn't ask God, what I had done wrong. Was I not a good enough mother? Did I love you too much? How could this Creator, the One who doesn't let a sparrow fall without knowing it, allow this to happen to you?

The anger I felt was frightening. Even weeks later, I wanted to scream out to Him, "What about the hopes and dreams we shared about her life? Was it for nothing that she worked hard and tried to do her best?" But I couldn't ask God anything, and the distance between us grew greater each day.

At night I wondered if you were scared in that moment you faced death. Did it hurt? Did you call out to me, but I wasn't there? During those weeks, I was never closer to going insane than as

I held your blouse close to my face and wept for hours at a time.

But, Sherry, now that you are ageless instead of only nineteen, perhaps you have the answers I may never have. There's so much we cannot know here on earth. Perhaps you knew, as I do now, that I was never truly alone. *God was where He had always been.* I was the one who had moved. I turned my back on Him because I couldn't bear the pain of living out my life without you, and He was the One I blamed for your death.

But this must not be a totally sad visit, my little one. We shared much joy together, and each memory is precious for it is all a part of us.

Mother love is very difficult to describe. I didn't love you the same way all the time. There were times I wanted to hold you close and protect you from all the hurts I knew you would encounter in life. But our love was also a companionable one. And how we did laugh and enjoy each other in your eighteen years. It was almost comical the way a glance from one of us could cause the other to dissolve into spasms of laughter when we least expected it.

And, Sherry, once in a great while, I would forget how much I loved you and become impatient with and critical of your teenage problems. I am so sorry for those times and thankful they didn't happen often.

Now it has been six months since your death and people expect me to be over my pain. Some friends are quick to say, "Oh, you're doing so well! I *knew* you would!" Or worse still, someone might comment on my bravery as though I had been in a battle of the flesh instead of one with the spirit. And, because it is more noble to act cheerful than to be sad, I pretend.

But now the pretending has become more real than reality, and I find myself caught up in the age-old quandary of hating to face the truth. One part of me recognizes that our life together is over and I have to go on. But another part of me cannot face the awful fact that you are never coming back. And I weep for that part of my life, and yours, that is ended.

How to reconcile those statements? I wish I knew. My only hope is that this question, as so many others have been, will be answered in God's own time.

Go back now, my darling. I have promised to put a time limit on our visit. But there is no limit on your space in my heart.

My Sherry, how very, very much I love you.

I never realized how much we can learn about life from death. We rush around at such a frenzied pace and then find ourselves unfulfilled when we get to where we are going. Too late, we learn that success is not a synonym for happiness and that fortunes alone can rarely fill the emptiness of our hearts.

The death of a loved one teaches us to search for goals that are long-lasting and to let go of certain values that used to be important. Our society thinks all questions can be solved quickly, computer-style, but sorrow makes it clear that some things are never answered and never solved. We have to learn to live with them.

When life is good, it is easy to believe that we are immune from any great loss if we pray hard enough and go to church and try to live in a morally acceptable way! But grief reminds us that the ultimate loss is death, and no one can escape. No matter how much medical science discovers or how many organs doctors learn to transplant, we will all eventually die. And everything we have ever been and all the relationships we have ever had will be frozen forever in that instant.

So what does it all mean? In my weaker moments, I wonder if there is any sense to our existing in the world. But Scriptures tell us all life is meaningful and, in my stronger moments, I hold fast to that hope. Surely, it would bring more sorrow to see a loved one lost to life than to death. That thought compels me to keep searching.

For the first time, I noticed in the Bible that Jesus doesn't say, *"In case* you have tribulation," or "You *might* have tribulation." He says, "Ye *shall* have tribulation" (John 16:33, italics added). And when I look around at friends, I see with new vision that no family is exempt from tragedy of one kind or another.

Even children, whom we think of as completely carefree, have worries that are shown in drawings as well as their play. We look at teenagers and see a glossed-over facade of gaiety, but nearly all are insecure and troubled. Young adults are anxious about getting ahead in the world, and the elderly are worried about finances, ill health, and being alone. No one ever escapes heartache except for brief periods, yet we stupidly think bad times in life are abnormal and undeserved.

The uncertainties of life make it hard to believe that your love for us is so great. *Why do bad things happen,* we wonder. But when we stop to consider the possibilities of a monitored and controlled universe, we see that restricting the lives of others takes away any likelihood of growth for them. It was out of love for mankind that you made us free to choose. We have the absolute freedom to choose our life-styles, our priorities, and our goals.

As the Master Planner, you could have created us as robots, programmed through instinct to always do your will. But you gave us the freedom to do your will by choosing to do so. And, of course, the only way we can have the choice of doing right is to also have the choice of doing wrong. This means that sometimes we go the wrong way. And, occasionally, our choices meet in a horrible tragedy. But to allow something to happen as a natural consequence doesn't mean you planned it or wanted it to be. Instead, it all comes back to us and the fact that we still have so much to learn.

It's ironic, when we look at the gospel, that we should measure you by what happens to us. Hollywood endings are not consistent with real life, and they most definitely are not consistent with the Cross! Our choice comes in deciding how to live with that truth. But our faith comes from knowing you are not an indifferent God, and our assurance comes in realizing that the one thing in life that never changes is your love.

I feel a new strength from somewhere. The nightmares have stopped, and my thoughts of Sherry are happier ones. The letter to her helped gather up the remnants of unfinished talks, and I have not wept or needed to pretend for several days. Yesterday I gave her lovely blouse to Herman. I think I can do without it now, and he can give it to someone who will wear it with joy, as she did.

Jennifer and Allison came to visit today, and I enjoyed their chatter and play. I feel more within myself now. For so long, I have been separated, not knowing how to get my mind and body back together again.

Now, when friends drop by, I smile, I talk of days to come, and I laugh. Perhaps not as joyous a laugh as I once had, but still a laugh. Occasionally, I go with them to shop and to meet other friends. They probably know that I still grieve, but rarely does it come into our conversation. And I accept that, for I have been places they have not been and felt pain they could not know.

Sometimes, remembering, I drift away and do not hear what is being said. But the moment passes, and I return to pick up the thread of talk and go on. Hour by hour, day by day, grace sufficient. Now I understand.

I am not the same, God, but I think I am on the way back.

I sat today with a woman whose son had just died. I did not know her, but a friend thought I could bring her comfort. It is hard for society to realize that, sometimes, there is no comfort. A grieving mother only wants her child back, and anything short of that is too little. Knowing this, I simply held her and we both wept, her for the loss of her son and me for the fact that I wanted to help and couldn't.

Did my eyes once look that dead and empty? I had not faced a mirror image of myself in sorrow, and the shock was devastating. But I won't forget. Her face will haunt me forever as that awful symbol of a ripped-apart world.

Be with her, God. The road through grief is so lonely. No one has traveled her particular road before, and the ground will be rough and full of pitfalls. Some travelers never find the way, and a few decide it is easier to join their children in death than to try. But most of us stumble along, filled with hurt and yet aware that our very existence is marked by a movement through time. No matter how hard we try, we can't hold on to the present. Moments, one by one, always disappear and become merely a part of the past.

There were times when I wanted to stop life. *Just let me savor this special joy or saturate myself with this fruit of my labors,* I would think. But I dared not try. There was so much to be seen, to be heard, and to be enjoyed. And, sadly, when my mirror turned inward, there was just as much to be lost, to be suffered, and to be endured.

Is it all part of your plan? Could it be that life is less rewarding when we don't experience both sides of truth?

Perhaps my calmness of the past few weeks precipitated Herman's talk with me today about cleaning out Sherry's bedroom. He explained that some mothers are a little hasty in putting away things that belonged to their dead children, but he added it was just as big a mistake to wait too long or not to do it at all.

I was horrified at his suggestion and did not hesitate to let him know. "What's wrong with leaving her room as it is? No one needs it, and I like seeing it the way she left it!"

"It's not healthy," Herman said. "It's almost as though you were expecting her to come back at any moment."

"That's not true!" I replied quickly. "Jonnie and I cleared some things out last fall!"

I was almost in tears when I suddenly jumped up and, motioning him to follow, ran down the hall to Sherry's room. I stopped at the door and surveyed the sun-swept room she had occupied. I had made the yellow ruffled bedspread, canopy cover, and curtains for her twelfth birthday, and she had lived here like a fairy princess through all the brightness of her teenage years.

"This was *her* room, and these are *her* things!" I stood like a mother tiger protecting her cubs and stared angrily into his eyes.

But Herman didn't answer. Irritated by his silence, I tried again, and louder. "Am I supposed to forget she ever existed? *How do you pack up a lifetime and put it away?*"

For once, Herman didn't offer any words of comfort, but strode purposefully into the bedroom. With a gesture that encompassed the whole room, he turned around and spoke in as loud a voice as I had used. "You take the canopy down! Put new curtains up! Buy a new bedspread! Paint the room! *Martha, this room is like a shrine to Sherry!* You can't live normally with this untouchable shell of a monument in your home! *You don't need it! She left you more than this!*" He reached out to touch my shoulder, but I drew back and sank down on the bed.

"I won't do it! *I can't!* It's the only thing left. The one last part of her life!" My body shuddered as I tried to make the thought take hold in my mind. My head was pounding.

I've done all I can, I argued defensively to myself. *Why should I have to give up everything left of my little girl?* Yet my conscience nagged me. Herman was leaving our church to become pastor to a church in Charleston, and I knew he wanted to help me take this one last step before he left.

With a sigh, he sat down on the bed beside me. "Don't agree or disagree yet," he urged gently. "There isn't a timetable that is perfect for everyone. Just promise to think about it. I think, in time, you will come to see it is not a *giving up* of Sherry, but a *letting go* of her."

But I wouldn't look at him. His eyes were saying things I didn't want to hear. So we sat for a long while, not speaking. And when it was time for him to leave, I was sorry because I felt I had let him down. In an even stranger way, I felt I had let Sherry down, too.

"Do you want to be healed?" Jesus once said to a lame man. A thought-provoking question but, perhaps, a very necessary one. Healing cannot come to us unless we want it enough to receive it.

Do I want to be healed? I ask that question today as I struggle to put away Sherry's belongings. And I know the answer is yes. Even though memories of her are in everything I touch, I want the gaping wound in my heart to be healed. So I must take this step to box up the parts of her that confuse reality, knowing her real legacy can have no limits.

I feel your nearness, God, and it strengthens me, but it wasn't always so. There were times when you were lost to me and I thought I would never find you again. My energy was all used up in pain, and I had none left to search for or feel anything.

How easy it was to feel your presence the night of Sherry's birth when I kissed her little face in joyous welcome! And how deserted and alone I felt the morning I kissed her good-bye when she lay still and silent in death.

I suppose, by the same token, it is easier to see your beauty in a glorious sunrise than in the ashes of a burned-out home or building. Yet you are there, as you are in all things of life. And with spiritual roots that are deep enough and strong enough, we grow to feel your presence and see your beauty once again.

Each of us lives in futile hope that the worst will not happen to the world that is ours. Very few people are prepared for tragedy. But once it happens, we have to decide. We can go on living, reaching out to others in a way we never could before. Or we can be destroyed, allowing the tragedy to claim still another victim.

Many times in the past months, I've doubted that I could ever thank you for my daughter's life without saying, "Thank you for Sherry's life, *but* . . . " I saw no way to reconcile her loss with being grateful for her life. I thought the only connector we had left was grief.

But I no longer live whole days in the past, as precious as those memories might be. Questions that tore at my soul are being answered, as they had to be, by my own rediscovered and renewed faith. And Herman's persistence in making me work through my sorrow has made me realize that tragedy alone could never defeat me. Only I could do that. The choice was always mine.

"Sometimes it's hard to understand the will of God," an older man murmured as he grasped my hand in the store today. I stiffened as I usually did whenever I heard this strange statement.

God's will for the world is not evil, but good, I wanted to say. It isn't ugliness, but beauty. And it certainly isn't tragic accidents for our precious children, but long productive lives lived in His service and for His glory. No, dear friend, what God wants for our lives is good, but what we choose is not always good. The whole scheme of life has been designed around freedom of choice, the greatest gift of love ever given to a created being. The problem comes because most choices we make involve people other than ourselves.

Think it through, my friend, for only then can we help others to see. Sherry rode back to the dorm with her friend. That was her choice. In the state's opinion, the girl was negligent in operating the car. A conscious or unconscious decision. And with the collision of two choices, we are left to live a lifetime of sorrow.

How presumptuous to blame that on God!

I was so sure I would go to heaven and be waiting when my children arrived. The horrible possibility of one of them going first never occurred to me.

Sherry's life was like an unfinished letter, stopped in the middle of a sentence. She was allowed no good-byes and given no words of love before she left. Yet the Bible tells me she is contented and, after months of searching, I believe this to be true.

I have lived so long in the world of indecision, God. The pressure of such a world can be torturous, but perhaps doubt has brought me closer to you than peace of mind could ever have done. When this most senseless of all things happened, you answered my cries by sharing the pain and quietly affirmed your presence, even in the depths of hell.

I learned to trust you in a new and absolute way. Things that were not visible to me before were suddenly clear. If I suffered over the tragedy of Sherry's death, then how much more you, who created her, must have suffered. And if I love her with such an abiding love, then how much more you, who bought her with your life, must love her.

There is a calmness when I think of her in heaven now. A grievous and quiet acceptance of something I cannot change. I would give everything I own for just one glimpse of her, but all the wanting in the world cannot make it so.

"I have set before you life and death," I read in Deuteronomy weeks after the accident. And, finally, after a long and tedious struggle, I have chosen life.

It's amazing how quickly we judge life by pain. Most of us think a painful life is a bad one and a pain-free life is a good one. But is life ever that simple? There are a few pleasures in even the worst of circumstances, and every joyous occasion has a touch of sadness about it. The mirrored premise again.

We can look at grief in the same way. When Sherry died, I was so crushed by sorrow that I became blind to life. But the very grieving itself made me see life more clearly, and the tears gave me a larger view of life to look upon. I saw pain and suffering as a universal common denominator and found, to my astonishment, that there is no real difference in people. There is only a difference in the scars they carry through life.

Is this why Jesus said we would know Him? Because He had scars, too?

Everything is beginning to make sense now, and the pieces seem to fit. I know some things about me will forever be changed but, at last, I no longer get angry when people make trite statements about God or suffering or death.

"Just remember, God never shuts one door without opening another," said a not-so-close friend in the store today.

God doesn't shut *any* doors, I wanted to answer her. It is *we* who do the closing, and not just doors, but hearts and minds as well. But it would have been pointless. And it wasn't her fault. So much of life has to be seen on the *inside* to be understood.

Little by little, a kind of peace is seeping into me, and I find the harsh pain gone and most of the anger soothed. Sometimes, grief forces us to redefine life and examine questions we had never had a reason to ask. And the answers bring out poignant self-discoveries we might never have known.

From the day we are born until the day we die, there will always be pain at having to relinquish precious and cherished things we cannot keep. But knowing the gifts are not permanent, would we give up the time they are ours to enjoy or even wish them away? And knowing we would not, I sat alone and, for the first time in a very long time, I wept.

And the tears were a way of saying good-bye.

Does Sherry dream, God? Does she ever think of us and our life together? I worried for so long that she did, but now I think not. At least, not in the homesick way I once feared. Instead, the assurance grows within me that she thinks of us only in terms of the future. The future of our life together.

It seems years ago—and only yesterday—that I sobbed to my brother, Tom, "How long do I have to go on living?" I couldn't move fast enough to close the distance that lay between Sherry and me. But now I know it is not meant for us to rush through life. The gift of being is far too precious to waste.

I wept so many tears for special times that would never be again. There was not enough strength in me to relinquish someone so cherished, something I felt belonged just to me. I forgot that, first of all, my daughter belonged to you.

The dawning of Easter. A celebration of life eternal. Dozens of Easter lilies adorn the altar, and the church is filled with the sound of trumpets and choirs and people. It is a day like no other in the Christian church as we rejoice in Christ's victory over death. A victory that has taken on a brand-new dimension for me.

My eyes fastened on the cross as the triumphant strains of music rang out. Such a beautiful symbol, but it really bears no resemblance to the wooden, man-made cross of Calvary.

"Christ is Risen, Alleluia!"

What a lonely, bleeding figure you must have been, Lord, and how abandoned you must have felt by man and God.

"Risen, our victorious Head!"

How sad it is that no one there knew they were watching the redemption of *all* people instead of the crucifixion of *one* man.

"Sing his praises, Alleluia!"

I wonder if it would have made a difference, Lord.

"Christ is risen from the dead!"

But it *did* make a difference! And I caught my breath as the great shining message of Easter was suddenly born again in my heart. *He is alive!* The thought was almost staggering in its intensity. He died and yet He lives! And in His life we shall live also! This was His promise. His word of hope. His power of Resurrection.

Dear God, let me never forget. Keep the promise of Easter in front of me always. Help me remember that I need not weep for a lost dream, a lost life for Sherry.

105

Because Christ came into the world and defeated death, she *does* live! And so must we.

Something happened to me today, and I am still trying to put it all together. Since Easter, I've spent hours trying to determine what makes a life complete. I knew it couldn't be explained by the number of years one lives because Jesus only lived thirty-three years, and His was the most complete life ever known.

Nor did I think it could be the accomplishments of a lifetime because very few people live long enough to realize all of their goals, and many children die without time to achieve anything. Would we dare say their lives are not complete? And what about the life of a brain-damaged or retarded person who can never be self-sufficient in even his most primary needs? Surely, the meaning of life has to be deeper than anything we can do.

But I could carry the thought no further and always stopped at that point. Life is your most cherished gift, and you *must* give all life meaning. But how?

The call came when I was folding clothes. A baby had died, leaving his young mother distraught with grief. Would I come and sit with her, a friend wondered. Of course I would.

"Tell me about your baby," I said softly as I sat down beside the young woman.

"He was so sweet," she wept, "so tiny and seemingly so perfect. We looked at him in anguish because he had such a short while to live. And yet we knew those precious few hours would change our lives forever!"

My own eyes filled with tears, and I reached for her hand. It was true. Their lives would be changed because that little one had touched them in a way that nothing else could. And wasn't this the answer I had been searching for? The answer

107

that had been there all along, waiting for me to reach out to it?

Every life affects someone or something! It's really simple. The meaning of life is found, not so much in what we do, no matter how good that may be, but rather in how we affect or change the lives of others. And isn't that the purpose of it all, God? That our being here *matters*?

Who can ever look back at life without wishing some things had been different? Is it our humanness that always yearns for more or aches for what might have been?

I face that moment today and know that the greatest sorrow of my life will be for Sherry and the fact that she died so young. I grieve because she was gifted and eager and open to life. I grieve for what she missed by not having the chance to fulfill her dreams. And I grieve mostly because she was mine and because memories of her can never be enough.

But the focus of my grief changed when I was suddenly catapulted into the past to stand at the foot of the cross on Easter morning. For the first time, I saw grief as the price we pay for love and, even though it hurts and it may always hurt, I would choose again to love. The greatest grief would be in never having had her at all.

Once I was angry that the world didn't stop when I did, but today I welcome the beauty of spring. It is a season that affirms life and a time for healing and for new beginnings. "Let not your heart be troubled," said Jesus, "believe." Only believe. And my heart is at peace.

I know that Christ has gone ahead to prepare a place for me. I believe He had prepared one for Sherry. And I am confident that He will prepare one for all believers. If it were not so, He would have told us.

The April sunset, so brilliant only a short while ago, has begun to fade. And still I sit, unwilling or unable to let the moment pass. What a long and sorrowful way I have traveled. And how surprised I am that my long journey has only brought me home to myself. And perhaps there was no other place for it to end.

You have heard so many cries of sorrow and shared so many tears of pain. Do you smile with me now as I begin my prayer? The prayer you have waited on for such a long time. The prayer that begins:

Thank you, God, for Sherry . . .

Thank you, God, for Sherry.

Thank you, God, for her loving nature and for her outgoing personality that broke down the thickest barriers between her and others.

Thank you, God, for her energetic brightness and for the flowers of love she planted in our hearts.

Thank you, God, for the love we shared as a family and for the special bond we had between us as mother and daughter.

Thank you, God, for trusting us with Sherry for eighteen years.

Thank you, God, for her baptism when she became one of your own.

Thank you, God, that she achieved her dream of becoming a college cheerleader.

Thank you, God, that for Sherry the mystery of dying is over.

Thank you, God, that she will never know heartaches again, but will abide with you in heaven where there is no pain or sorrow.

Thank you, God, for loving me, being patient with me, understanding my hurt, and forgiving my anger in blaming you for Sherry's death.

And most of all, God, thank you for the gift of your Son, Jesus Christ, who promises us eternal life with Him and with all those who die in Him. I can rest now and let her go, knowing we will be together again in your kingdom forever.

Amen.

About the Author

Martha Bittle Clark lives in Charlotte, North Carolina, and is active in The Compassionate Friends, an organization for bereaved parents. She has earned a history degree from the University of North Carolina in Charlotte and enjoys substitute teaching. Active in her church, she has interests in writing, playing tennis, gardening, going fishing with her husband Cecil, and attending every basketball game she can. She spends much of her time talking and working with bereaved parents, feeling that this is a ministry God has given her.